THE CHILDREN'S BOOK OF
WILDLIFE WATCHING

THE CHILDREN'S BOOK OF
WILDLIFE
WATCHING

WRITTEN BY DAN ROUSE

DK

Contents

Introduction

Wildlife is all around us: bees fly from flower to flower, frogs hop in and out of ponds, birds nest high in trees, and mice burrow beneath our feet. If you start paying more attention to wildlife, you'll discover that animals and plants all have different features, habits, and skills— and you can learn about these just by watching.

You can help wildlife, too. Creatures need safe places to live, breed, eat, and drink. There are lots of different ways you can be kind to wildlife by offering plants and animals what they need. And because the wildlife around you is all connected in an ecosystem, helping one living thing can positively impact the wider environment— and the planet as well! Are you ready to learn more about wildlife? Come on, let's go!

What is wildlife?

Wildlife is all the animals, plants, and fungi that are found in a place. Everywhere, including green spaces near you, contains wildlife that either visits or lives there.

Did you know?

Native species are plants and animals that have been part of the wildlife of an area for thousands of years.

Ladybugs are seen on plants in summer, and hibernate in winter.

Changing with the seasons

Wildlife species may change throughout the seasons. Common species that spend their whole year in a place are known as "residents." "Migrants" are species that spend a certain amount of time in one area and the rest of the year in another.

Power plants

Plants make food by combining energy from the sun with moisture and nutrients from the soil. Without plants, all wildlife would be lost. They offer nectar and food to pollinators and birds, all-important cover and water for many animals, and when they decompose they provide nutrients in the soil.

Moss is an important plant for amphibians, such as this American toad.

Eastern bluebird

A bluebird relies on caterpillars for food.

Natural balance

To truly support wildlife, we have to care about all wildlife—not just the species we like. All wildlife exists in an ecosystem, and if we remove one species, it can affect other plants or animals in the ecosystem.

Caterpillar of the eastern tiger swallowtail butterfly

Some people might see caterpillars as pests, but they are important to their ecosystem.

Types of wildlife

Each chapter in this book looks at a category of wild creatures. This page offers a glimpse into the amazing range of wildlife found in green spaces.

Think about it!

When you look at a green space, some creatures can be spotted more easily than others. Can you think why this might be?

Eastern bluebirds fly south to southeastern US or Mexico for the winter.

Birds

A huge variety of bird species visit green spaces. Some birds are in the garden all year round, and these are joined by others that migrate in spring and fall.

Minibeasts

Minibeasts include insects, such as beetles, flies, and bees, and other creatures without a backbone, such as worms, millipedes, and spiders.

Mammals

Mammals include mice, rabbits, foxes, badgers, and bats. The simplest definition of a mammal is a warm-blooded animal with a backbone, which (usually) gives birth to live young.

Reptiles

Reptiles are cold-blooded, which means that they cannot produce their own body heat. Instead they bask in sunny spots, gaining warmth and energy from the sun. There are two main groups: snakes and lizards.

This Colorado River toad is an amphibian.

Amphibians

Also cold-blooded, amphibians include frogs, toads, and newts. These little creatures start life as aquatic animals. As they mature and develop lungs, they move onto land.

Day and night

While some animals are often seen during the day, other animals emerge at night in order to avoid the hot sun or to find food.

Think about it!

Diurnal animals are often the most familiar. Why do you think this might be?

Chickadee

Peacock butterfly

Daytime

Animals that are active during the day are known as diurnal. Reptiles sit and soak up the sun. Bees, butterflies, and other insects feed on nectar. Most birds are diurnal, too.

Cloudless sulphur butterfly

Earthworm

Top tip

Wildlife is usually most active in spring and summer, so it will be easier to spot animals during warmer months.

Bumblebee

Barred owl

Raccoon

Night-time

Animals that are active at night are known as nocturnal. Raccoons, foxes, and owls are common nocturnal animals, but many minibeasts come out at night, too.

Red fox

Dawn and dusk

Dawn and dusk is when we may see some wildlife looking for their last feed before sleep, or emerging from their daytime slumber. Animals that are active during this time are known as crepuscular.

Bat

Yellow underwing moth

On the hunt

Some animals come out as darkness falls for food. Bats hunt crepuscular insects, while moths visit flowers that open at night.

Reproduction

Insects look for crevices in which to breed and plants on which to lay eggs, while amphibians spend time in the water mating and laying spawn. Mammals may burrow in a bank or under a hedge to make homes in which to raise their young.

Shelter and feeding

Wild creatures use shelter for warmth, to rest, make nests and homes, and as a place to find food. Animals that eat other animals often move quickly to catch their meal. All animals need water to survive, so often seek it.

Frogs mate and lay eggs underwater.

Animals in action

Although different species have different behavior, the reason behind their actions is often shared. Animals usually take action when they are searching for food, water, and shelter, or when socializing, staying safe, or reproducing.

Staying safe

Most animals move away from danger if they feel threatened; they may also be camouflaged to avoid being spotted. Hibernation is one way that many species survive the winter cold.

This garter snake will move fast to catch its food.

Did you know?

Sometimes, an animal's actions can help other living things. Birds, for example, eat berries and spread the seeds in their droppings.

Fox cubs often play in order to learn new skills.

Socializing

Wild animals often come across each other, and we can watch what happens. Some species are territorial. Robins, for example, fiercely defend their territory from other robins. Different calls and behaviors may also help animals attract a mate.

Food chains

A food chain is a way of explaining how food (and energy) passes through a group of species. The simplest way of looking at a food chain is in terms of the producer, the consumer (or prey), and the predator.

Think about it!

Food chains include: herbivores (plant eaters), carnivores (animals that eat other creatures), and omnivores (animals that eat both plants and animals). Which of these categories are you in?

Primary consumers are often insects, like this milkweed beetle.

Producers

Plants are the basis of most food chains. Plants use energy from the sun, along with carbon dioxide from the air and water, to make their own food.

Primary consumer

The primary consumers are herbivores feeding on plants. They are often insects, but can be mammals or birds. These species are often food for large predators further up the chain.

Frogs eat insects, such as flies.

Apex predators

These are creatures that do not have a predator, but instead eat only species lower down the food chain. Examples include birds of prey, which eat consumers such as garden birds and small mammals.

Secondary consumer

Small mammals, reptiles, amphibians, and birds typically eat the primary consumers. Some minibeasts prey on others. For example, spiders eat flies, and some beetles eat smaller insects.

Decaying matter can be harmful. Never touch any decaying matter.

Nutrient cycle

After wildlife dies it decays, releasing nutrients back into the soil so they can be used again by plants to grow.

Life

Death

Decay

Green spaces

Gardens can be a safe space for wildlife. No matter how small or large the space, we can encourage more wildlife to visit and even stay. By focusing on what wildlife needs to survive—food, water, and shelter— we can alter our green spaces to work harder for wildlife.

An unwild garden

Small elements in a garden can make it unfriendly to wildlife, even if the garden looks similar to one where wildlife thrives.

Top tip

Choose plants that pests don't like, and you won't need to use chemicals to protect them. That's good news for other wildlife.

Chemicals used on plants, such as pesticides, are dangerous to wildlife.

Plastic lawns and plants are of no use to wildlife.

Real grass offers food sources and shelter.

Wild vs unwild

Some green spaces are more wildlife-friendly than others. Some simple changes to a garden can encourage more wildlife. These factors can be the difference between a wild and unwild space.

A wild garden

Although it might need a little more care, a garden that is friendly to wildlife can be more rewarding for all.

A helping hand

A wild garden is not just about letting a variety of plants grow freely, or creating wilder areas. Other things can be done to make a space more friendly to wildlife, such as bird houses.

In a smaller or paved space, hanging baskets and pots attract insects, which then attract birds and even bats.

An access hole in a fence allows creatures without wings to move freely through barriers.

Wilder areas can give animals a safe space to hibernate.

A variety of plants is good for animals.

A water source is vital for birds, mammals, and insects to drink from and bathe in.

Food and drink

Wildlife is naturally attracted to green spaces that provide both food and water. These can come from a number of different sources.

Finding food

A successful garden ecosystem needs good food sources: decaying wood, plants, algae, and soil.

Woodpeckers find their insect food in tree trunks. They also eat oozing sap, acorns and nuts, and tree frogs.

Every bit of a plant can be a source of food: flowers, leaves, and grasses.

Algae and tiny organisms are the basis of diets for many water-dwelling creatures, such as tadpoles.

Soil contains nutrients for both plants and some minibeasts, like earthworms.

Finding water

Like humans, wildlife needs to drink often, as well as keep clean. A natural environment provides a variety of water sources for wildlife to use.

Damp or boggy areas can be a great source of water for animals.

Dew droplets and raindrops offer tiny pools of water for small animals to access.

Wildlife doesn't just get moisture directly from water, a lot of it comes from natural food sources, such as berries.

Additional sources

Green spaces thrive when natural food and drink sources are available. However, additional food and water sources can help them flourish.

Bird baths are a great extra water source. Low bird baths allow insects and other animals to use them, too.

Ponds not only provide a home for creatures, some animals drink from and clean in them.

Feeders for small mammals and birds can provide a much-needed meal.

23

Safe shelter

Safety is important for wildlife. Many species will only visit an area if they feel secure. Shelter allows wild creatures to feel safe from predators, particularly when they are breeding. Different species use different places for shelter.

In the trees
For singing and surveying for food, birds will perch high up to look around. For nesting, they look for a more sheltered spot.

Hedges and shrubs
Hedges, shrubs, and climbing plants offer shelter for insects in bad weather and a perch for birds visiting a feeder.

Grass and flowers
Insects will hide among plants so they cannot be seen. Evergreen plants stay green all year round, so provide shelter across all seasons.

Soil and leaves
Small mammals prefer to avoid all predators, so will burrow beneath the soil or make dens among fallen leaves.

Rocks and stones
Reptiles choose an open place to bask in the sun, but with a space to rush to should a predator or risk emerge.

Red-winged blackbird

Did you know?

A good shelter must have enough cover, but still allow the wildlife to observe their surroundings.

American robin

Rabbit

Northern cardinal

Dragonfly

Five-lined skink

Plant life

Plants are wildlife, but they can also offer a lot to other wildlife. Gardeners often keep the wider ecosystem in mind when planting greenery.

Layers of plants

Not all plants grow and live in the same space. Plants can be separated into layers, with each layer contributing differently to an ecosystem.

1 **Trees**
Trees provide the top layer of plants and offer shade, shelter, and food to insects, birds, and some mammals.

2 **Shrubs and climbers**
The upper-middle layer of plants is likely to be mainly shrubs and climbing plants.

3 **Plants for the sun**
Many plants like sunny spots. These areas are most likely to be visited by pollinators.

4 **Plants for the shade**
Shady areas of vegetation are vital for minibeasts as well as some amphibians and small mammals.

5 **Grass**
Longer grass at the edge of a lawn offers shelter and food for insects and their predators.

Balconies

Flying insects and birds visit balconies, making regular stops if there is food or shelter for them. Bird feeders and nectar feeders can make a balcony more wildlife-friendly.

Small spaces

Not all green spaces are big. A small garden can offer plenty of opportunities to encourage new species of wildlife to visit.

Paved areas

In a paved garden, containers can be used for plants. Containers that are light and easy to move are best. Grouped containers, making a larger area of green in layers, helps wildlife to move and shelter among the pots.

This balcony is packed with plants on different levels. It offers shelter and damp corners for wildlife to hide in.

Sharing spaces

Green spaces aren't just used by wildlife, they are appealing to humans and pets, too. When thinking about green spaces, it can also be worth considering the wider environment.

Predator risk

Cats and dogs are predators by nature. Cats in particular are a danger to birds and small mammals. Pet owners can look for ways to reduce the risk to wildlife without affecting the pet's quality of life.

Wood and biodegradable materials are alternatives to plastic.

Top tip

A bell on a cat's collar will make a sound when the cat moves, warning birds or mammals that the cat is nearby.

Plastic-free

Plastic causes problems in the environment and can be a danger to wildlife. Avoid making the problem worse by using alternatives to plastic in your garden.

An insect hotel offers shelter for many species.

Did you know?

Some gardeners work together to create pollinator corridors so insects can move easily between gardens.

Super spaces

Many previously common species are in decline. Gardens can help their numbers to grow by offering a safe place for wildlife to eat and shelter.

Staying safe

It's always best to have an adult with you if you are active in a garden. Stay clear of compost bins and ponds to avoid disturbing creatures and hurting yourself.

You will need:

Pen **Notepad** **Plain paper**

Design a wild space

Planning is a very important part of creating a green space. Why don't you try designing your own? Be sure to consider the wants and needs of those that'll use it.

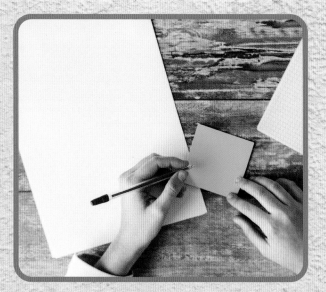

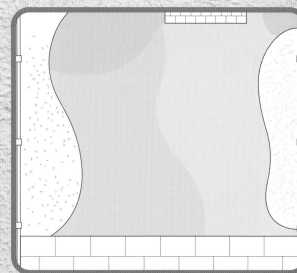

1. List the needs

Think about what you would like to use the space for, such as a lawn for playing sports.

2. Sketch your outline

Draw a rough plan of your space. Include the different types of ground you'd like to have—flower beds, short and longer lawns, and any patio areas.

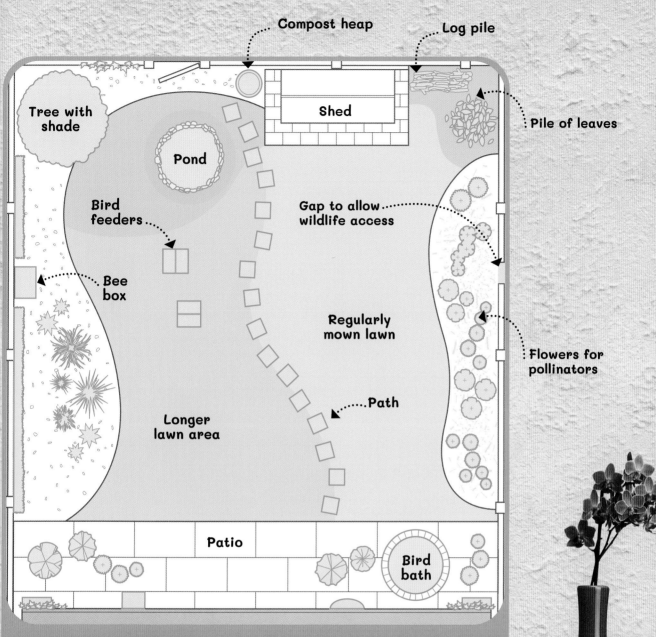

Compost heap

Log pile

Tree with shade

Shed

Pile of leaves

Pond

Bird feeders

Gap to allow wildlife access

Bee box

Regularly mown lawn

Flowers for pollinators

Longer lawn area

Path

Patio

Bird bath

3. Add the detail

This is just a plan, so you can be as creative as you like! Focus on the key elements for wildlife: food, water, and shelter. Also think about access—try to avoid creating obstacles for animals entering and leaving your green space.

Minibeasts

Minibeasts range from insects, such as bees, butterflies, and beetles, to the less glamorous creatures, such as worms, slugs and snails. They are an important group of species, and are also known as invertebrates, meaning an animal without a backbone.

Insect life

Insects are different from other minibeasts like worms or slugs. They have three pairs of legs, two clear body segments, and usually one or two pairs of wings. Insects include butterflies, bees, ants, and beetles.

Think about it!

Insects play an key role in helping plants reproduce by pollination. Without insects we wouldn't have many of the plants we eat.

Life cycle of an insect

Many insects have a number of stages in their life cycle.

1 Eggs

Many insects, including butterflies, moths, bees, ants, and beetles, lay eggs.

2 Larva or caterpillar

Eggs hatch to produce larvae (or caterpillars in the case of moths and butterflies).

3 Pupa or chrysalis

The larva or caterpillar feeds and grows until they form a pupa or chrysalis.

4 Adult

An adult insect emerges from the pupa or crysalis, usually looking completely different from the larva.

Pupas are an inactive form of the insect.

Visiting flowers

Bees, butterflies, moths, and beetles are all pollinators. They visit flowers to feed on nectar, and some gather pollen as a protein source. Different flowers attract different pollinators.

Flat flower head

A flat flower head, such as dandelion (above), sunflower, or apple blossom, is easy for pollinators to access.

Tubular flowers

Foxgloves (above) have a large circular opening into a tube that pollinators crawl into. Lavender is also tubular, but pollinators access it with their tongue.

Double flowers

Some roses (above), are bred to have double flowers filled with petals. These may not contain nectar, and if they do, pollinators can't access it.

Did you know?

Insects take pollen from plant to plant as they visit flowers—it often collects on hairs on their bodies and rubs off on other flowers.

35

Garden minibeasts

Not all invertebrates are pollinators—but all have a vital role to play in the garden ecosystem. Woodlice, slugs, snails, and worms are found all over gardens and green spaces.

Green darner

Ladybug

Water hoglouse

Around water

Some minibeasts are found in and around ponds and pools. Adult dragonflies and damselflies thrive above water; they lay their eggs in the water and hunt smaller insects above the surface.

Among the flowers

Predatory ladybugs eat aphids on flower and plants. Spiders create webs among pollen-rich flowers where they wait for flies to become trapped.

Ladybugs are a type of beetle. Depending on the species, they can have spots, stripes, or no markings at all.

Garden spider

Common true katydid

Reddish-brown stag beetle

Banded Snail

Woodlouse

Common earthworm

In the leaves

Minibeasts thrive in leaf litter and log piles. Hunters lurk among the leaves waiting for their prey. Slugs and snails also search for food under leaf litter.

Underground

Decomposers break down decaying matter in soil. Worms consume and break down rotting plants. Woodlice and beetles eat wood and decaying plants.

Minibeast habitats

Minibeasts need shelter at all stages in their lifecycle. Plants and other garden features are vital for many minibeasts to nest in, burrow in, hibernate, lay their eggs, and shelter their pupae.

Wild variety

The best green spaces offer a wide range of habitats where minibeasts can make themselves at home and hide from heavy rain and predators.

Mixed plants

 Dense, bare, tall, and short vegetation allows a variety of minibeasts to thrive.

 Ideal for: Butterflies, spiders, earwigs.

Ground level

Many insects lay their eggs in soil, while invertebrates burrow underground. Some bees nest in grass.

Ideal for: Ants, beetles, worms, slugs, bumblebees.

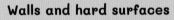

Trees

🏠 Many minibeasts live and breed within trees, mainly in crevices and gaps in the bark.

🐞 Ideal for: Earwigs, woodlice, centipedes, millipedes, tree bumblebees.

Decaying wood

🏠 Fallen logs and other dead wood provides a great habitat and shelter.

🐞 Ideal for: Spiders, beetles, woodlice, worms, slugs, snails, millipedes.

Walls and hard surfaces

🏠 Walls can provide a home to minibeasts in crevices and holes.

🐞 Ideal for: Spiders, ladybugs, masonry bees, mining bees.

Top tip

Although some bees dig into buildings, they do not create serious damage, so don't remove them.

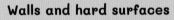

39

You will need:

Clear pot   Soft paintbrush   Magnifying glass   Plain paper   Pencil

Studying minibeasts

If you've ever lifted a stone or moved a plant pot, you'll have seen some minibeasts. By recording the minibeasts you find, you can build up a picture of what creatures are in your area.

1. Locate and collect

Identify habitats and watch minibeasts. To collect a minibeast, gently sweep it with a soft paintbrush into a clear pot. Do not use your hands, as this can transfer oils and toxins onto the minibeast's body.

2. Identify

Take a close look at the minibeasts you have collected. Try to indentify the species using this book or other resources.

Never handle minibeasts directly, and always ask an adult for help.

3. Add the detail

Record the species you've found, taking notes or pictures. Release the minibeasts gently where you found them; avoid keeping them for more than about five minutes. Consider sharing your findings with a local wildlife group.

Research it!

Which of your small visitors do you like best? Choose a minibeast that you've seen near your home and try to find out more about it. Research everything you can think of:

- What it looks like
- Size
- Diet
- Any noises it makes
- Habits
- Likes and dislikes
- What else can you think of?

With a little research, you can become an expert!

Minibeast profiles

Use these profiles to help identify some of the bugs you might see near your home.

Drone fly

A type of hoverfly with brown and orange markings on a dark body.

Length ½—1 in (12—25 mm)
Habitat Widespread, including gardens
Favourite food Nectar from ivy

Common eastern bumble bee

Black and yellow bee with a circular patch of black in the middle.

Length ½—1 in (12—25 mm)
Habitat Forests, wetlands, urban areas
Favourite food Pollen, nectar

American bumble bee

Black bee with two patches of yellow on upper and lower pars of the body.

Length ½—1 in (12—25 mm)
Habitat Widespread, including prairies
Favourite food Pollen, nectar

Augochlor pura

Shiny and brightly colored; usually green, but sometimes copper, gold or blue.

Length ⅓ in (8 mm)
Habitat Forests, fields
Favourite food Pollen

Bee-fly

A family of flies with a long proboscis (mouthpart) and two wings.

Length ½ in (12 mm)
Habitat Gardens, woodlands, cliffs
Favourite food Many different nectars

Yellow hair extends down body

Two-spotted bumble bee

This bumble bee looks very similar to the common eastern bumble bee.

Length ½–1 in (12–25 mm)
Habitat Forests, farmland, fields, gardens
Favourite food Pollen, nectar

Tricolored bumble bee

Black bee with yellow and orange on its body, giving it its tricolored name.

Length ½–1 in (12–25 mm)
Habitat Woodlands, wetlands, fields
Favourite food Pollen, nectar

Honey bee

Bee with a dark upper body, and striped lower body. It has large black eyes.

Length ½–⅔ in (12–18 mm)
Habitat Widespread, including gardens
Favourite food Pollen, nectar

Painted lady butterfly

Butterfly with white spots on the forewing, and a row of black dots on the hindwing.

Wingspan 2—2½ in (50—63 mm)
Habitat Widespread, including prairies
Favourite food Nectar-rich plants

Luna moth

Moth with a gray body, orange and brown wings, long antennae, and a long proboscis.

Wingspan 3—4½ in (76—115 mm)
Habitat Forests, suburban areas
Favourite food They have no working mouths!

Eastern black carpenter ant

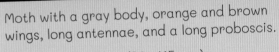

Dull black ant with whitish or yellow hair, especially around the abdomen.

Length ¼—¾ in (6—21 mm)
Habitat Widespread, including urban areas
Favourite food Butterfly and moth larvae

Common garden snail

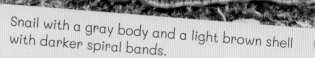

Snail with a gray body and a light brown shell with darker spiral bands.

Shell diameter 1¾ in (45 mm)
Habitat Hedgerows, gardens, urban areas
Favourite food Decaying plant matter

Reddish- browntag beetle

Yellow markings

Garden spider

Large, reddish-brown beetle with large jaws. Males slightly larger than females.

Length ¾—1¼ in (20—36 mm)
Habitat Forests
Favourite food Tree sap, rotting wood

Spider of varying colours, between dark gray, brown, orange, and even yellow.

Length ⅛—⅝ in (4—18mm)
Habitat Hedgerows, woodlands, gardens
Favourite food Flies, butterflies, wasps

Common earthworm

Seven-spot ladybug

Worm that's brownish-purple above its swollen, orange saddle; pinkish-yellow below.

Length 8—10 in (200—250 mm)
Habitat Soil
Favourite food Decaying plant matter

Beetle with bright red wing casings and seven black spots.

Length ¼ in (6—7 mm)
Habitat Gardens, meadows, parks, hedgerows
Favourite food Aphids

45

Reptiles and amphibians

Reptiles include lizards and snakes, while frogs, toads, and newts are all types of amphibians. Reptiles prefer to bask on warm soil or rocks, while amphibians need boggy areas and water in which to breed. Both look for locations full of minibeasts for them to hunt.

Reptile and amphibian habitats

Reptiles and amphibians are cold-blooded, so they must seek heat from their environment. Reptiles find warm areas to bask in, whereas amphibians spend time on land and in water.

Water snakes sometimes look in ponds for a meal. ......

Northern watersnake

Where are the reptiles?

Reptiles are mainly seen between March and October when the sun's heat is at it's strongest. They often rest in the day and hunt in the evening and at night.

Rocks retain heat, ... so they are used by reptiles to bask in the sun.

Some snakes are dangerous, so always stay a safe distance from them.

Water attracts water snakes, which swim and hunt for prey. ......

Thick vegetation ...... offers a refuge for lizards and snakes.

Compost heaps attract snakes, which like the warmth and to eat minibeasts.

Eastern glass lizard

Reptiles search for a meal in piles of leaves.

Logs in a sunny spot make a suitable basking place for lizards.

Five-lined skink

Garter snakes like to hunt in thick vegetation.

Garter snake

Where are the amphibians?

Like reptiles, amphibians rely upon the environment for their heat, but they are able to spend time on land and in water. They tend to be slower moving, and live in cooler and damper areas.

While reptiles love to bask on logs, amphibians prefer to live around the logs, with many enjoying the damp and dark decaying matter under and within log piles.

Amphibians aren't fussy creatures, and some species, such as newts and frogs, can be found in tiny ponds and ditches.

Amphibians love damp areas, such as beneath stones and rocks, boggy areas, and wetlands, or simply damp areas of the yard.

Reptile and amphibian life

Both reptiles and amphibians feed on similar foods: mainly insects and other invertebrates. Even the smallest fly is a source of food. However, they're attracted to slightly different spaces for shelter.

On the hunt

Amphibians hunt on land and in water, while reptiles hunt mainly on land and are faster to dart out and catch their prey. Amphibians usually feed every two or three days, while snakes might eat only once a week.

Hunting each other

Grass snakes hunt for toads and frogs within a pond and are quite nimble in water. Newts also hunt tadpoles and spawn in the pond.

A toad makes a good meal for a garter snake.

Hunting mammals

Some snakes feed upon mice and voles. Venomous snakes use two fangs at the front of its mouth that inject venom to help paralyze their prey.

Hunting minibeasts

Frogs and toads feast upon flies, and eat other insects such as dragonflies. Lizards, frogs, newts, and toads hunt for slugs and snails. Lizards also catch flies and crickets.

Creating a home

Amphibians often seek cool, damp spaces where they can rest during the day, leaving them at night to hunt. Reptiles seek shelter with warmth to give them energy to hunt in the daytime. We can help these animals find a home with a few simple shelters.

Frog and toad home

A small house made of wood or ceramic in a damp area will provide a space for reptiles and amphibians to shelter within. A tile in the corner of a space will provide similar shelter.

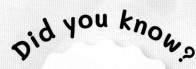

Did you know?

Grass snakes lay their eggs over the summer. This means it's a good idea not to disturb compost heaps during this time.

There are some houses designed specially for amphibians.

Reptile matts

This is simply a metal sheet or piece of sturdy fabric, such as burlap, that warms up and provides a dark space underneath.

Compost bins

The conditions in a compost bin are warm, damp, and dark—a great location for amphibians and reptiles, such as snakes and slow worms, to rest.

You will need:

 Net

Light-colored trays

Magnifying glass

Notebook

Pond dipping!

Ponds contain more than amphibians and their young. They are often full of tiny creatures, too. Pond dipping is a great way of studying all the different creatures in a pond, from the tiny insects to the larger amphibians.

⚠️ Do not go pond dipping without an adult, and remember that some ponds are protected and should not be disturbed.

Top tip

The best time to pond dip is during spring and summer, when wildlife is normally most active. Fewer creatures will be seen in winter.

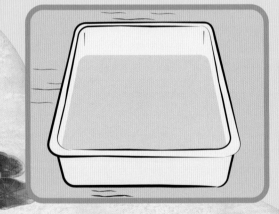

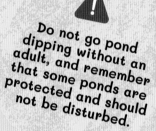

1. Prepare the trays

Fill the trays with pond water. Pale-colored trays allow you to see any creatures more clearly.

Be careful near the edge of water.

2. Gather some creatures

Use a net to scoop out some water creatures from an area of the pond and quickly turn out the net into a tray. Try to separate predators and prey into different trays.

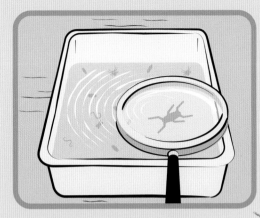

3. Look closely

Once you've placed the creatures in a tray, use a magnifying glass to try to work out what wildlife you've found.

4. Return the creatures

Don't let the water and the creatures heat up in the sun. Note down the creatures you've found, or take a picture if you can, and gently let them back into the water where you found them.

Hidden creatures

Some pond creatures hide in vegetation, or plants, when people are near. Gently taking them out to observe allows us to take a closer look at species, such as newts, frogs, and toads.

Red-spotted newt

Not all animals should be caught; this newt is poisonous.

Reptile and amphibian profiles

Use these profiles to help identify some of the reptiles and amphibians you might see near your home.

Common watersnake

Brown, gray, black, or even red snake. Dark blotches across the body resemble bands.

Length 24—54 in (61—137 cm)
Habitat Rivers, lakes, ponds, marshes
Favorite food Fish, amphibians

Garter snake

Dark brown, gray, or black snake, usually with three light-colored stripes.

Length 18—54 in (46—137 cm)
Habitat Widespread, including forests
Favorite food Amphibians

Eastern glass lizard

Legless lizard, that can break its tail into several pieces when under threat.

Length 18—43 in (46—109 cm)
Habitat Woodlands, wetlands
Favorite food Insects, spiders

Common five-lined skink

A dark-colored lizard with five yellow or white stripes running down its body.

Length 5—9 in (127—216 mm)
Habitat Forests
Favorite food Insects, spiders

Wartlike bumps

American toad

Brown toad, with wartlike bumps down the back and sides and horizontal pupils.

Length 2–4½ in (51–144 mm)
Habitat Widespread, including suburban areas
Favorite food Insects

Eastern newt

Yellow, brown, or olive-green newt with spots, and a tail flattened sideways.

Length 2½–5 in (64–127 mm)
Habitat Lakes, streams, marshes
Favorite food Insects, worms

Red-backed salamander

Dark brown, black, or bluish salamander with a long red stripe down its body.

Length 2–4 in (56–102 cm)
Habitat Forests
Favorite food Insects, worms

Green frog

Frog that is various shades of green, with a white belly.

Length 2–4 in (51–99 mm)
Habitat Ponds, lakes, swamps
Favorite food Insects, newts

Birds

Common in green spaces, birds are easier to spot in winter when branches are bare and they are seeking food. However, they are easiest to hear in spring, when they sing to stake a claim to their territory and attract a mate.

Birds through the year

Birds behave differently across the seasons due to when they breed and the amount of food available. Some even migrate—traveling across continents, often north and south, with the seasons.

Wood thrush

Mourning dove

American robin

American goldfinch

Spring

Birds sing at this time to attract a mate, as well as to claim their territory. They also gather nesting material.

Summer

Chicks hatch and grow their adult feathers. Parents gather food for them.

Welcoming birds

Some birds, such as chickadees, are in the garden all year. Migratory birds, such as wood thrushes, visit for summer or winter. By leaving grass and hedges longer, green spaces can be more welcoming all year round.

Tufted titmouse

Black-capped chickadee

Fall

Young birds reach adulthood and some migrate, while others arrive in search of berries. Birdsong is rare.

Winter

Birds look for shelter in trees and shrubs, and food from fruit and minibeasts.

Birds' food and drink

Both food and water are vital to birds' survival. Depending on the species, birds look for food in different places. It is also possible to add more food to local green spaces.

Food sources

Different types of bird feed at different levels in the garden. Some use plants as a food source, while others prey on small animals. Feeders also provide an extra food source.

Seedheads on plants are full of nutritious seeds. Birds also feast on tree fruits and nuts.

Some birds eat minibeasts. Birds of prey hunt mammals, reptiles, amphibians, and other birds.

Feeders or feeding stations provide food for lots of bird species.

Tell your friends

If your friends have access to a green space, encourage them to hang a feeder or put in a bird bath for the local birds.

Water sources

Water is important for birds for drinking, and also for cleaning themselves. Birds dampen their feathers to remove any parasites, bacteria, and dirt.

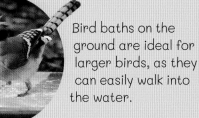

Pond edges are a great place for birds to drink and stay clean. A gentle slope of stones allows birds of different sizes to enter the water.

Bird baths on the ground are ideal for larger birds, as they can easily walk into the water.

Raised bird baths are best for smaller birds. They are best placed close to trees and shrubs, so birds have somewhere safe to escape to.

Trees

Tall trees offer shelter as well as a place to sing in spring. Larger bird species, such as pigeons, may nest high in trees.

Black-capped chickadee

Taller plants

Plants such as lavender, tulips, and sunflowers can help small birds to move around safely and offer shelter.

American goldfinch

Shelters and nests

Shrubs, climbers, and trees are fantastic natural shelter and nesting locations for birds. The more varied the plants, the better, to give birds more nesting options as well as more food sources.

Think about it!

Which of these plants do you think would fit in a smaller or paved space, and be useful for nesting or sheltering birds?

Shrubs

Shrubs provide shelter when birds are foraging and visiting feeders, and birds may nest in larger shrubs.

Climbers

Climbers fit into all but the smallest of spaces. Some are dense and offer shelter and nesting places.

Purple finch

Small plants

These provide a place for birds to hop in and out when hunting and finding nesting material.

Northern cardinal

Plants in containers

Containers of flowering plants can be grouped together to give birds a refuge when startled.

63

You will need:

Build a nest

Robins and blackbirds are adaptable when nesting. You can make a simple bowl-shaped structure for them to nest in.

Don't use scissors without adult supervision.

Always wash your hands thoroughly after touching mud.

1. Remove loose items

Remove any hanging items from your sieve or colander, such as mesh that could break, tags, or any hoops that birds may get caught in.

2. Line the colander

Add a layer of wet mud to the inside of the sieve, pressing it down to create the basic shape of the nesting bowl.

Tell your friends

Let your friends know they can make a nest for birds in their garden. If they don't have an area to put a nest, it is also possible to make your own bird feeders.

3. Add nesting materials

Weave some nesting materials into the outside of the sieve. You will need an adult's help to do this.

4. Position your "nest"

Find a suitable place in your garden, with plenty of cover, and wedge the nest in place securely. Then ask an adult to attach it to the tree with garden wire or twine. Make sure that no sharp ends are sticking out.

Bird profiles

Use these profiles to help identify some of the birds you might see near your home.

Black-capped chickadee

This chickadee has a black head and throat, white cheeks, and gray back and tail.

Length 5 in (13 cm)   **Wingspan** 7 in (18 cm)
Habitat Forests, urban areas
Favorite food Caterpillars, spiders

American goldfinch

Males have a yellow body with a black forehe and wings. Females are olive brown.

Length 5 in (13 cm)   **Wingspan** 8 in (21 cm)
Habitat Grasslands, suburban areas
Favorite food Seeds

Blue jay

Bright blue bird with a white lower body. Long tail and black ring around the neck.

Length 11 in (28 cm)   **Wingspan** 15 in (38 cm)
Habitat Forests, urban and suburban areas
Favorite food Nuts, seeds

Purple finch

Males are red on their head, with white on their lower body. Females are brown.

Length 5½ in (14 cm)   **Wingspan** 9½ in (24 cm)
Habitat Woodlands, forests
Favorite food Seeds, berries

Crest on
the head

Northern cardinals
also have a crest

Tufted titmouse

Pale gray bird with a white belly and face. It has large black eyes and pointed crest.

Length 6 in (15 cm)   **Wingspan** 9 in (23 cm)
Habitat Woodlands, forests, suburban areas
Favorite food Ants, caterpillars

Northern cardinal

Known as the "redbird," the male is bright red all over. Female is reddish-olive in color.

Length 8½ in (22 cm)   **Wingspan** 11 in (28 cm)
Habitat Forests, gardens
Favorite food Seeds, insects, berries

Dark-eyed junco

Birds with a gray or brown head, breast, back, and wings, and a white belly.

Length 6 in (15 cm)   **Wingspan** 8½ in (22 cm)
Habitat Forests, parks, gardens
Favorite food Seeds, insects

Eastern bluebird

Males have a blue back and and orange breast. Females are duller with gray upper parts.

Length 7 in (18 cm)   **Wingspan** 12 in (30 cm)
Habitat Widespread, including woodlands
Favorite food Insects, spiders, worms

House finch

Adult males have a red face and breast with a brown back, while females are brown all over.

Length 5½ in (14 cm) **Wingspan** 9 in (23 cm)
Habitat Widespread, including woodlands
Favorite food Buds, fruits, seeds

Rose-breasted grosbeak

Males have a striking red breast, white belly, and black head and back. Females are brown.

Length 8 in (20 cm) **Wingspan** 12 in (30 cm)
Habitat Woodlands, forests
Favorite food Insects, fruit, seeds

American robin

Plump bird with a tuneful song. Males have a reddish-orange breast. Females are duller.

Length 10 in (25 cm) **Wingspan** 14 in (36 cm)
Habitat Widespread, including parks
Favorite food Worms, caterpillars

American crow

Large, stocky bird that is black overall, including its bill, legs, and feet.

Length 18 in (46 cm) **Wingspan** 37 in (94 cm)
Habitat Widespread, including parks
Favorite food Insects, frogs, worms

Downy woodpecker

The smallest woodpecker, it is white and black, and the male has a red patch on its head.

Length 6 in (15 cm) **Wingspan** 11 in (28 cm)
Habitat Woodlands, parks, gardens
Favorite food Insects

.....Small head

Mourning dove

A slim dove, mostly pale, with gray and black wings. Small, round head with black spot.

Length 12 in (31 cm) **Wingspan** 18 in (46 cm)
Habitat Widespread, including parks
Favorite food Seeds

Red-bellied woodpecker

Woodpeckers with a striped back, pale belly, and a red crown on the head.

Length 10 in (25 cm) **Wingspan** 17 in (43 cm)
Habitat Forests, parks, gardens
Favorite food Insects, nuts, fruit

Wood thrush

Reddish-brown thrush with a white, speckled belly and pink legs.

Length 8 in (20 cm) **Wingspan** 14 in (35 cm)
Habitat Forests
Favorite food Insects

Mammals

From big badgers and foxes to tiny
voles and mice, mammals are a large
and varied group. They visit most
green spaces but may be hard to spot.
Rural areas are likely to see a wider
range of mammals, but there are
plenty to be seen in urban areas, too.

Where to find mammals

It can be hard to spot mammals in green spaces. Some are small, and most are good at avoiding being seen so that they can keep safe from predators. But if you know where to look, they can be easier to find.

Mammal life

Like other animals, mammals enjoy and use different parts of gardens and green spaces.

1 Trees

Squirrels are good climbers, and they eat, breed, and nest in trees. Smaller mammals, such as mice and voles, will look for nuts and seeds in trees.

2 Stones and rocks

Stone walls are a vital habitat for weasels. With their long, slim bodies, they are able to squeeze into small gaps.

3 Vegetation

Small mammals, such as voles and rabbits, move between plants looking for food and safety.

4 Underground

Holes near the base of trees, shrubs, or hedges are likely to be entrances to burrows for mice or rabbits.

Brown rats look for food mainly at night.

Winter

Winter is a difficult time as there is little food, and it takes a lot of energy to keep warm. Some mammals hibernate, while others become less active to save energy. However otters and foxes increase their hunting.

Night life

Many mammals are nocturnal. Mice, voles, and shrews have sensitive noses and whiskers for sensing danger. Mice have large eyes with big pupils to help them see well in the dark. Voles and shrews don't see well, but have very sensitive hearing.

Top tip

When spotting mammals, it's often easier to see traces, such as footprints, a burrow, or remains of food, rather than the animal itself.

Mammals' food and drink

Mammals have a wide variety of food sources, depending on their size and diet. Just like humans, they also need water to survive, too.

Food sources

Food can be easy to find for smaller mammals. Larger mammals roam farther to find food, and may visit gardens to feed.

Squirrels and other small mammals look for trees that drop nuts. Berries are eaten by mice and voles, and sometimes foxes.

Nuts and berries

In the soil

Small mammals search for slugs and snails to eat. For moles, earthworms are an important food source.

Low-growing plants

Stems, flowers, leaves, and bulbs may all be nibbled by mammals. They can be especially attractive to rabbits and hares.

Hunting other animals

Weasels and American martens hunt for mice and voles, and somtimes birds, too. Foxes will eat pigeons and rats.

In the water

Ponds can provide fish and amphibians for otters to eat. The insects that live near water provide a steady food source for bats.

Ponds

Ponds are a great water source. Larger mammals, such as badgers and foxes, as well as small ones, will come here to drink.

Water sources

Mammals get some water from their food, but also need other water sources.

75

Mammal habitats and shelters

Mammals need shelter, in particular during the breeding season and for warmth during colder months or to hibernate. Small mammals that are often hunted by larger animals need a safe place all year round.

Hedges

Hedges form barriers, with plenty of shelter, but still allow wildlife, such as foxes, badgers, and hedgehogs to pass through. Rabbits and other mammals often dig burrows under hedges.

Compost heaps

Mammals thrive in spaces such as compost heaps. Worms and slugs use compost heaps for feeding, making them great hunting grounds for many mammals.

Think about it!

Smaller species of mammal tend to have more offspring than larger mammals. Can you think why this might be?

Trees

Squirrels nest in trees, while the base of some trees provides a great place for mammals to create burrows and dens, as the soil is often looser around the tree roots.

Burrows and dens

Some mammals, such as foxes, dig a den or burrow. Underground is a safer place to give birth to young. Here, predators can't smell or hear their prey as easily.

Bats

The only flying mammals, bats are very smart, with an incredible memory for places. They can be seen flying over gardens at dawn and dusk. Different species have different hunting heights and methods.

Mexican free-tailed bat

High in the sky

Hoary bats tend to fly high, normally over the tops of trees, chasing down flying beetles and moths. Mexican free-tailed bats also flutter among the tree canopy, catching insects.

Mid-level

Big brown bats tend to fly slowly among the trees, searching for beetles. Northern long-eared bats fly just below the branches of trees, capturing insects.

Low to the ground

Bats such as pallid and silver-haired bats are often seen "hawking" (chasing their prey) close to the ground. They focus on insects, including moths. Pallid bats even walk on the ground.

Did you know?

Bats use echolocation, which involves making a sound wave that bounces off objects, returning an echo.

Pallid bat

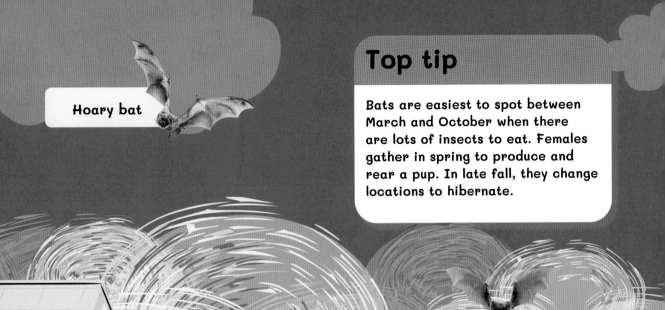

Hoary bat

Top tip

Bats are easiest to spot between March and October when there are lots of insects to eat. Females gather in spring to produce and rear a pup. In late fall, they change locations to hibernate.

Northern long-eared bat

Big brown bat

Silver-haired bat

You will need:

Tray   Sand   Food

Mammal tracker

It's often hard to spot mammals that are nocturnal or move under cover. Creating a mammal tracker will help you identify the species that visit your garden.

Check food labels to make sure that you aren't allergic to any of the ingredients and don't eat the food yourself.

1. Prepare the tray
Pour some sand into the tray and smooth it with a straight edge. Spray it with water to dampen it.

2. Position the tray
Add some food to the center of the sand, such as seed mix, and place the mat under some cover (for example, beside a hedge).

Top tip

Try placing the tray in different areas of the garden to compare how often each area is visited. Experiment with different animal-friendly foods, too.

Observe it!

Look for chew and bite marks on surrounding leaves, or droppings and pellets. These could be additional evidence of mammals in the area.

3. Identify the tracks

Enticed by the food, mammals will come and go, leaving their tracks. Here the larger tracks belong to a squirrel and the smaller ones to a mouse.

Mammal profiles

Use these profiles to help identify some of the mammals you might see near your home.

Deer mouse

Gray to brown mouse with a white belly and white feet. Tail is very long.

Length 6 in (16 cm)
Habitat Prairies, grasslands, woodlands
Favorite food Seeds, fruits, spiders

Meadow vole

Brown vole ranging in shades from gray to red with a white belly.

Length 6 in (16 cm)
Habitat Grasslands, fields, marshes
Favorite food Grasses, grains

Eastern chipmunk

Rodent with light brown fur on upper body, with five dark stripes along the back.

Length 10 in (25 cm)
Habitat Forests
Favorite food Seeds, nuts, insects

Gray squirrel

Squirrel with mainly gray fur, but browner fur on feet and face. It has a long, fluffy tail.

Length 10 in (26 cm)   **Tail** 9 in (23 cm)
Habitat Parks, gardens, forests
Favorite food Seeds, nuts, flower buds

Weasels have rounded ears. ⋯⋯⋯⋯

Long-tailed weasel

Short-tailed weasel

Weasel with long, tubelike body with short legs. Typically brown with a lighter belly.

Length 14 in (35 cm)
Habitat Woodlands, fields, marches
Favorite food Mice, rats, squirrels

Weasel with a very long, slim body with short legs. They have brown fur with a white belly.

Length 28 cm (11 in)
Habitat Woodlands, grasslands, wetlands
Favorite food Voles, shrews, rabbits

Groundhog

Eastern mole

Also known as a woodchuck, it has a rounded body, brown fur, and short legs.

Length 20 in (51 cm)
Habitat Woodlands, fields
Favorite food Grasses, bark

Moles have very dark gray, velvetlike fur, with pink feet and a pink nose.

Length 5 in (13 cm)
Habitat Grasslands, woodlands
Favorite food Worms

Little brown bat

Small bat with medium-brown fur, and darker fur on the ears and wings.

Size 3 in (8 cm)   **Wingspan** 9½ in (24 cm)
Habitat Forests, usually near water
Favorite food Insects

Big brown bat

A bat with various shades of pinkish tans to reddish and rich browns.

Size 5 in (13 cm)   **Wingspan** 11 in (28 cm)
Habitat Widspread, including urban areas
Favorite food Insects

Eastern cottontail

Small mammal with long ears and long hind legs, gray fur, and a white fluffy tail.

Body length 16 in (41 cm)
Habitat Widespreads, including grasslands
Favorite food Grasses

Opossum

Mammal with gray fur on the body and light gray face. It has a thick body with short legs.

Body length 30 in (76 cm)
Habitat Swamps, woodlands, urban areas
Favorite food Small mammals, reptiles

Foxes have black-tipped ears.

Fox

Doglike mammal, with red—orange fur, white on the underbelly, and black socks on the feet.

Length 31 in (80 cm)
Habitat Widespread, including urban areas
Favorite food Small rodents

American Badger

American badgers have a light gray, stocky body with short back legs.

Length 30 in (75 cm)
Habitat Grasslands
Favorite food Gophers, squirrels

River Otter

Otters have brown fur, a thin body, small ears, and a thick tail, ideal for swimming.

Length 24 in (61 cm)
Habitat Rivers, wetlands, estuaries
Favorite food Fish

White-tailed deer

Large hoofed mammal with brown fur and a white belly. Males have large antlers.

Length 75 in (191 cm)   **Height** 36 in (91 cm)
Habitat Woodlands, prairies, swamps
Favorite food Grasses, nuts, buds

Watching wildlife

There are plenty of ways to improve your experience in green spaces, from looking for tracks and traces, to photographing or filming species as they pass through. You may also want to share the fun with others by joining wildlife groups and activities.

Tracking wildlife

You can learn to spot clues that different animals have visited an area. Identifying footprints, droppings, and other traces are ways to get to know the visiting wildlife without disturbing it.

Chew and bite marks

Nibble and chew marks help us to identify which species are visiting an area. Slugs and snails may eat whole leaves, but smaller species, such as caterpillars, partially remove the leaves. It's possible to see marks of beaks or teeth chew marks on larger fruits.

Birds make holes in fruit with their beaks.

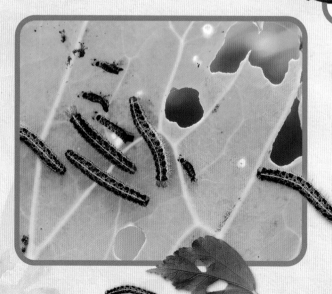

Did you know?

Butterflies lay their eggs on particular leaves, as many types of caterpillar often only eat one or two types of plant.

Droppings and pellets

It might seem gross to study what animals leave behind, but droppings and pellets can tell us a lot. Looking at droppings allows us to observe what wildlife has been attracted to our space. For example, herbivore droppings are often drier and larger than carnivore droppings.

Do not touch animal droppings or pellets—they might contain harmful bacteria.

Droppings are small and round.

Pellets are the undigested remains of food coughed up by some birds.

Footprints

It's easier to see footprints in damp mud or sand, and in snowy conditions, than on dry soil and in areas of vegetation, so winter is an ideal time to start tracking. You can practice your identification skills in a local garden or green space.

These footprints are from a pigeon.

Community wildlife

Wildlife watching can be a hobby you do alone,
but it's worth looking to see if you can find and
join a community that shares your enthusiasm,
whether that's in school, your
local area, or online.

Community groups

Many areas have groups
that share your enthusiasm
for wildlife, including local
bird clubs and natural
history groups. Nature
reserves often have
conservation groups that
you can join. Keep an eye
out for posters in your local
library or ask an adult to
look through community
pages online for you.

Do not attend
community groups and
local events without a
trusted adult, and use
online forums with
adult supervision.

Online information

Often online groups specialize in certain wildlife and are a great source of knowledge, where people post their first sightings of migrant birds or unusual species. With the help of an adult, you'll be able to find out all sorts of information and stories about your favorite wildlife.

Local events

Something you may find hugely rewarding is going to or organizing local events. There are several wildlife themed weeks and days across the year, such as Moth Night, International Dawn Chorus Day, and Mammal Awareness Week that all deserve attention.

Meet the author!

The author of this book, Dan Rouse, turned her love of wildlife into a job. She spends a lot of time making green spaces wildlife-friendly, and talking about wildlife on the TV and radio.

Is there any wildlife you're especially interested in?

Birds are my true passion, but as I have watched them over the years, I have appreciated more and more that without the many other species involved in the ecosystem, they would not be able to thrive.

Black-capped chickadee

Brown squirrel

What attracts you to green spaces?

My garden is my refuge. When the world gets a bit too much, there's nothing like having lunch outside listening to the birds and watching the squirrels perform their acrobatics trying to reach the feeders.

What is the main message of this book?

We may think we have to travel to special reserves to see wildlife, but it's possible to get much more familiar with nature closer to home: in our gardens and green spaces.

Do you have any early memories of wildlife in your local area?

I remember as I was growing up being excited to watch the bats hunting around the garden hedges and tree line. Even now, 20 years later, I still get excited and stop everything to watch hedgehogs out in the garden, or look among the flowers to find out which butterflies prefer the flower species that I've planted.

Do you have any final thoughts?

Wildlife can and will adapt to any given space, so let's share our gardens through the year with wild companions, and enjoy living with the snuffling of mice, the gentle songs of birds, and the buzzing of bees.

"Even the smallest area can be transformed for a host of species to enjoy."

Glossary

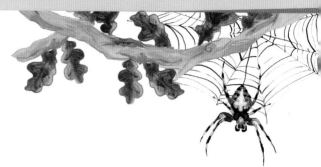

Bask Lie exposed to warmth or light

Camouflage Blend in with the surroundings

Carnivore An animal that feeds only on other animals

Compost Natural materials that have decayed. When added to soil, compost helps plants grow better

Consumer A living thing that eats other livings things for energy

Crepuscular An animal that is active at dusk or dawn

Decompose Break down into smaller parts

Diurnal An animal that is active during the day

Ecosystem Group of animals and plants that live and interact with each other in one area

Habitat The natural home of a plant or animal, such as a pond

Herbivore An animal that feeds only on plants

Hibernation When a living thing spends an extended period inactive during winter

Invertebrate An animal without a backbone

Larvae Young insects that have hatched from eggs, but haven't yet turned into their adult form

Migrate Move to a different continent or climate as the seasons change

Nocturnal An animal that is active at night

Nutrient A chemical in food that helps animals and plants to grow and thrive

Omnivore An animal that feeds on both plants and other animals

Pellet Small ball or piece of something

Pest A living thing that harms crops or livestock

Pesticide A substance that is used to destroy pests, such as aphids

Pollination The transfer of pollen between flowers for fertilization

Predator An animal that hunts other animals

Proboscis In insects, a long, sucking mouthpart

Producer A living thing that creates its own food

Resident An animal that lives in the same location all year

Shrub Plant that is like a tree but smaller, with leaves close to the ground

Territorial Protective of their space

Index

Editor John Hort
US Editor Jill Hamilton
US Senior Editor Shannon Beatty
Senior Art Editors Ann Cannings, Kanika Kalra
Assistant Art Editor Nishtha Gupta
Senior Picture Researcher Sakshi Saluja
Production Editor Becky Fallowfield
Production Controller Leanne Burke
DTP Designer Sachin Gupta
Managing Editor Jonathan Melmoth
Managing Art Editors Diane Peyton Jones, Ivy Sengupta
Publishing Coordinator Issy Walsh
Delhi Creative Head Malavika Talukder
Art Director Mabel Chan
Publishing Director Sarah Larter

Illustrations by Abby Cook

MIX
Paper | Supporting
responsible forestry
FSC™ C018179

This book was made with Forest
Stewardship Council™ certified
paper – one small step in DK's
commitment to a sustainable future.
Learn more at
www.dk.com/uk/information/sustainability

Acknowledgments

Dorling Kindersley would like to thank Amy Pimperton for proofreading, and Helen Peters for the index.

Discover more nature at www.danrouse.org.uk/kidscorner

Picture credits

The publisher would like to thank the following for their kind permission to reproduce their photographs: (Key: a-above; b-below/bottom; c-center; f-far; l-left; r-right; t-top)

1 Dreamstime.com: Isselee (bc). Alamy Stock Photo: Phil Degginger (cra); proxyminder (tr). 2 Alamy Stock Photo: Wendy Johnson (br); Oleg Rodionov (bc). Dreamstime.com: Howard Cheek (ca); Wanda Prapan (cl); Yasonya (bl). 3 Alamy Stock Photo: Jim Laws (cra/Lotus corniculatus). Dreamstime.com: Goldutlan (ftr); Mikhail Strogalev (cars); Lightpoet (bc); Techa Tungateja (fbr). Getty Images / iStock: E+ / Chushkin (tc). Shutterstock.com: Ivan Chistyakov (cra). 4 Dreamstime.com: Dusena (bl/ Butterfly); Alamy Stock Photo: Tabor Chichakly (tc). 5 Alamy Stock Photo: Jared Hobbs / All Canada Photos (br); Pete Oxford / Minden Pictures (b). 6 Dorling Kindersley: British Wildlife Centre, Surrey, UK (bc). 7 Alamy Stock Photo: blickwinkel / F. Hecker (cla); Michael Durham / Nature Picture Library (tc). 123RF.com: Roman Zwerver (bc). Dreamstime.com: Elena Sineglazova (b/ Nuts); Rudmer Zwerver (tr). 8 Dorling Kindersley: Stephen Oliver (3xPebbles). Dreamstime.com: Musat Christian (ca). 9 Dreamstime.com: Maria Aleshina (tl); Steve Byland (cr); David Havel (cb); Jefunne Gimpel (tr). 10 Bonnie Barry (cl); Steve Bylanc (cb); Paul Reeves (cb); Tommason (br/Leaves). 10—11 Dreamstime.com: Dusena (Butterfly). 11 123RF.com: Anatolii Tsekhmister (cb). Alamy Stock Photo: Pete Oxford / Minden Pictures (cl); Terry Mathews (cra). Dreamstime.com: Natalya Aleksahina (cb/ berries); Scottpayne (cc); Melinda Fawcer (cb); Mikhail Blajenov (bl); Pinich Neelkun (bl). Getty Images / iStock: jskiba (tc). 12 Alamy Stock Photo: Phil Degginger (clb). Dreamstime.com: Roman Ivaschenko (bc); Roman Ivaschenko (cb); Brian Lasenby (c); Mikhail Strogalev (c/butterfly); Manfred Ruckszio (crb). 13 Alamy Stock Photo: Theo Douma / AGAMI Photo Agency (cra). Dreamstime.com: Harry Collins (tl); Isselee (bl); Cosmin Manci (crl); Cosmin Manci (cr). Dreamstime.com: Martin Grossman (cla); Lev Kropotov (l); Tanes Ngamsom (cr). 14—15 Dreamstime.com: Rawpixelimages (b). 15 Dreamstime.com: Teekaygee (tl). Getty Images: Moment / Carlos Carreno (br). 16 Dreamstime.com: Le Thuy Do (bl); Jason Ondreicka (cra). 19 Dreamstime.com: Irina Onufriev (br/Paper); Le Thuy Do (tr). Getty Images: Mary Ann McDonald (cl). 18—19 Alamy Stock Photo: Skip Moody / Dembinsky Photo Associates / Alamy. 20 Dreamstime.com: Alexander Maksimov (br); Ronniechua (crb). 21 Alamy Stock Photo: Ellinnur Bakarudin (ca); Art Phaneuf (cb). Dreamstime.com: Gerald Deboer (clb); Mrehssani (cb); Isselee (clb); Elena Nikolaeva (cb/Rain pink worm). 123RF.com: Ron Rowan / framed1 (cr). 22 Alamy Stock Photo: Morley Read (bl/Tadpoles). Dreamstime.com: Natalya Aleksahina (r/Berries); Matt Cuda (cb) Vaclav Volrab (tl); PeterWaters (tl/Bee); Nikhmkulov (cla); Prapat1120 (bl); Nikolay Antonov (b/2xWorm); Elena Nikolaeva (bl); Sarah2 (cb). Getty Images / iStock: E+ / jskiba (tr). 22—23 Dreamstime.com: Andreykuzmin (bc); Dmytro Synelnychenko (Texture); Viacheslav Voloshyn (Wood background). 23 Alamy Stock Photo: Ronny Rose (cla); Dreamstime.com: Tracy Immordino (cla); Stevenrussellsmithphotos (clb); Kevin M. Mccarthy (ca); William Wise (cla/ frog); Andreykuzmin (tc); Nikmenkulov (bc). 24 Dreamstime.com: Harold Stiver (cra). 25 Dreamstime.com: Charles Brutlag (cb); Ronniechua (cla); Dennis Donohue (clb); Scottpayne (crb); Melinda Fawer (cb/Dragonfly). 26 Dorling Kindersley: Frank Greenaway / Natural History Museum, London (3xButterfly). Dreamstime.com: Natalia Bachkova (clb). Venus Kaewyoo (l). 26—27 Dreamstime.com: Verastuchelova (t). 27 Alamy Stock Photo: Cary Clarke (cra). Getty Images / iStock: mtreasure (cr). 28 Depositphotos Inc: sanddebeautheil (clb). Dreamstime.com: Steve Byland (cra); Christopher Freeman (cla); Techa Tungateja (fbl); Lightpoet (bc); Somjring Chuankul (cb); Enika (clb/Pot); Chernetskaya (crb/Pots); Rixie (tr). Shutterstock.com: Ivan Chistyakov (bl). 28—29 Dreamstime.com: Melinda Fawcer (cb/3xLeaf); Pinich Neelkun (Bushes); Lev Kropotov (cb/Grass); GreenFine (cb/Fence). 29 Alamy Stock Photo: Wendy Johnson (bc/Pot); Oleg Rodionov (bc). Dreamstime.com: John Biglin (tl); Ivkuzmin (cl); Pinich Neelkun (clb/Bushes); Peter Titmuss (clb); Tracy Vickers (bl); Yasonya (br); Wanda Prapan (cr). Getty Images / iStock: Nerthuz (crb/Swing). 30 Dreamstime.com: Ilya Genkin / Igenkin (cla); Tetiana Komchatnykh (cla/Plant); Syda Productions (clb). 30—31 Dreamstime.com: Smileus (bc). Getty Images / iStock: zoom-zoom. 31 Dreamstime.com: Britishbeef (crb/Pebble); Viktoriia Kulish (crb/Orchid, crb); Mario Elias Munoz Valencia (crb/Notebook); Pictac (bc/Pencil). Getty Images iStock: VasilyKovalev (bc). 32—33 Dreamstime.com: Paul Reeves. 34 Dorling Kindersley: Frank Greenaway / Natural History Museum, London (br/Butterfly). 35 Dreamstime.com: Taya Johnson (r). Getty Images / iStock: ueuaphoto (tl). Shutterstock. com: Ole Schoener (clb). 36 Alamy Stock Photo: Manfred Ruckszio (clb). Dreamstime.com: Alekss (cb/Ladybird); Melinda Fawer (cl); Wirestock (tl); Palex66 (cb). 37 Dreamstime.com: Isselee (cra, clb); Larisa Lofitskaya (cla/Ladybug); Aleksander Kovaltchu (cb); Wayne Mckown (ca); Natalie Schorr (cla); Tsekhmister (cr); Zestmarina (crb). 38—39 Dreamstime.com: Cougarsan; Melinc Fawver (2xLeaf); Bert Folsom (Background). 38 Dreamstime.com: Anton Starikov (bc/Soil). Shutterstock.com: Andi111 (bc); Karyn Honor (cr). 39 Alamy Stock Photo: Jess Merrill (bl). Dreamstime.com: Gutescu Eduard (tl). naturepl.com: Rod Williams (cra). 40 Dreamstime.com: Andreykuzmin (r); Pelfophoto (tl); Pelfophoto (tl/Pencil); Nikolay Antonov (r/Worm); Anton Starikov (br/Bowl). Getty Images / iStock: Umesh Chandra (tl/Cup). 40—41 Dreamstime.com: Sharpphotos. 41 Dreamstime.com: Andreykuzmin (tr/Soil); Pockygallery11 (cra); Foton64 (tr). 42 Alamy Stock Photo: Bryan Reynolds (clb); Clarence Holmes Wildlife (cla). Dreamstime.com: Olha Lucenko (cla); Paul Reeves (cra). 43 Alamy Stock Photo: Arterra Picture Library (cra). Dreamstime.com: Julie Feinstein (cra); Ava Peattie (cla); Seksan Wangjaisuk (clb/Background); NatmacStock (clb). 44 Dreamstime.com: Guantana (cra); Ava Peattie (cla); Isselee (clb, crb). 45 Imagebroker / Arco / J. Fieber (clb). Dreamstime.com: Nadezhda Bolotina (r); Wayne Mckown (cra); Jason Ondreicka (cla). Getty Images / iStock: Geobacillus (crb). 46—47 Dreamstime.com: Tracy Munson. 48 Dreamstime.com: Brian Lasenby (cr). 49 Alamy Stock Photo: Gillian Pullinger (ca); Gay Bumgarner (bc); Anton Sorokin (cr). Dreamstime.com: John Anderson (c); Jason Ondreicka (cla); Steve Byland (cl); Melinda Fawver (bl). 50 Alamy Stock Photo: Gay Bumgarner (bc); Don Johnston_IH (cr). Dreamstime.com: Lev Kropotov (cla); Colin Temple (cl/snake); Photo2008a (bl). 51 Alamy Stock Photo: Joseph Chung (cra); Gillian Pullinger (br). Depositphotos Inc: sanddebeautheil (crb). Dreamstime.com: Lev Kropotov (r). 52 Dreamstime.com: Igor Terekhov (tl); Steve Byland (tc); Terracestudio (r). 53 Alamy Stock Photo: Bill Gozansky (cra). 54 Alamy Stock Photo: Andrew DuBois (cla, crb). Dreamstime.com: Iulian Gherghel (cra); Jason Ondreicka (clb). 55 Alamy Stock Photo: Robert Hamilton (cra); Jared Hobbs / All Canada Photos (clb). Dreamstime.com: Steve Byland (cla, crb). 56—57 Getty Images / iStock: ablokhin. 57 Alamy Stock Photo: Harju Alexandru Cornel (cra); Ondej Prosick (bc). 58 Alamy Stock Photo: Oleh Honcharenko (cra). Dreamstime.com: Steve Byland (clb); Zakharovaleksey (ca); Ronniechua (br); Michael Mill (cla). 59 Alamy Stock Photo: Lee Hudson (cra); Justin Kase zsixz (tl). Dreamstime.com: Vasyl Helevachuk (crb); Mikelane45 (tl); Nature Photographers Ltd (r/Woodpecker). 60 Dreamstime.com: Victor L. Almgren (cr); Steve Byland (tr, bc); JustNatureChannel (cr/American Robin); Moose Henderson (crb); Charles Brutlag (br); Wirestock (clb); Howard Cheek (c); Tsekhmister (clb/Worms); Prapat1120 (bl). Getty Images / iStock: E+ / jskiba (Berry branch). 60—61 Dreamstime.com: Natalya Aleksahina (Berries). Dreamstime.com: Tomason (3xDry Leaves); Julius Costache (cb/Grass); Vlarvix (tl). 61 Alamy Stock Photo: blickwinkel / F. Hecker (cla); Daybreak Imagery (cla/Woodpecker); Ivan Kuzmin (ca); blickwinkel / S. Gerth (ca/Sturnus vulgaris); Doris Dumrauf (bc). Dreamstime.com: Gerald Marella (cla); Ivonne Wierink (cl); Jgade (cb/Bird food); Stephencoyle (cla/Feeder); Richharnett (clb/Blue Bowls); Tsekhmister (ca/Worms); Pavel Mitrofanov (clb/Nuts); Elitsa Lambova (clb/Bowls); Chinook203 (cl/White Breasted Nuthatch); Pinich Neelkun (clb/Bush); Shashin Vardhave (bc/pot); Brian Kushner (crb); Getty Images / iStock: AtlasStudio (cb). Shutterstock.com: Evelyn Joubert (clb/Birds bathing). Getty Images / iStock: Andi Edwards (cb/Bird bath); Melinda Fawcer (cla/Leaf). 62 Alamy Stock Photo: Tabor Chichakly (cra). Dreamstime.com: Steve Byland (bl). Getty Images / iStock: CathyDoi (tc). 63 Dreamstime.com: Petr Jilek (tc/moss); Edward Westmacott (tc); Gerald Marella (cla/Bird); Rimglow (tc/Soil); Chatsuda Sakdapetsiri (tl/Sieve). Shutterstock.com: MINI (tr). 66 Alamy Stock Photo: Tim Zurowski / All Canada Photos (cla). Dreamstime.com: Richard Smith (clb). Dreamstime.com: Brian Lasenby (cra). 67 Alamy Stock Photo: George Ostertag / agefotostock (clb). Dreamstime.com: Bonnie Barry (cb); Michael Mill (cla); Ed Guthro (cra). 68 Dreamstime.com: Steve Byland (crb); Petar Kremenarov (cla); Wildphotos (cra); Ramblesan (clb). 69 Matt Cuda (clb); Gregg Williams (cla, cra); Harold Stiver (crb). 70—71 Alamy Stock Photo: Allen Wildlife Photography (r). Dreamstime.com: Isselee (crb); Rudmer Zwerver (cra). 72 Dreamstime.com: Dennis Donohue (clb); Dalia Kvedaraite (cla); Photo2008a (bl). Shutterstock.com: Ghost Bear (c). 73 123RF.com: Rudmer Zwerver (bl). Alamy Stock Photo: Papilio / Philip Marazzi (br). Dreamstime.com: Elena Sineglazova (bl/Nuts); Rudmer Zwerver (cla). 74 Dreamstime.com: Oksana Ermak (bl); Natalia Zakharova (tl/crb); Freeskyline (t Berries); Maya Kovacheva Photography (crb/Bowl). Getty Images / iStock: Guiyuan (cl). 74—75 Dreamstime.com: Tashka2000. Getty Images / iStock: rusm (Paper). 75 Alamy Stock Photo: Joe McDonald / Steve Bloom Images (crb). Dreamstime.com: Laimdota Grivane (c); Katerina Solovyeva (tl); Max5128 (cra); Maya Kovacheva Photography (c/Bowl); Alexandr Kononenko (bl). 76 Alamy Stock Photo: Simon Colmer (c); imageBROKER GmbH & Co. KG / P. Henry (cr). Dreamstime.com: Melinda Fawer (ca/Leaf); Swkunst (bl); Howard Cheek (r). Dreamstime.com: Anne Coatesy (crb). 76—77 Dreamstime.com: Tulius Costache (ca/Roof); Maximiliane Wagner (Background). 77 Alamy Stock Photo: Fox mother with kits by the den (crb); Wendy Johnson (cle Pot); Oleg Rodionov (ca/Petunia). Dreamstime.com: Svetlana Foote (cla); William Wise (cl); Lightpoet (cra/Squirrel); Lev Kropotov (r). Getty Images / iStock: Yasonya (cra). 78 Alamy Stock Photo: Rick & Nora Bowers (tr); Michael Durham / Minden Pictures (cm). Dreamstime.com: Melinda Fawver (tl/Leaf). 79 Alamy Stock Photo: Michael Durham / Minden Pictures (l, cra, crb); James Hager / robertharding (cra). Igor Yegorov; Anton Starikov (cla/Sand). 80—81 Dorling Kindersley: Stephen Oliver (Pebbles). 82 Alamy Stock Photo: Mike Lane (crb); Joe Blossom (cla). Dreamstime.com: Redfinch (clb); Melinda Fawver (bc). Science Photo Library: John Mitchell (cra). 82—83 Dreamstime.com: Tomason (b/Leaves). 83 Alamy Stock Photo: Jill Cooper (cla); Arto Hakola (cla); Ron Erwin / All Canada Photos (clb). Dreamstime.com: Tchana (crb); James Hager / robertharding (cra). Dreamstime.com: Paul Reeves (cra). 85 Alamy Stock Photo: Arterra Picture Library / De Meester Johan (cla); Arco / G. Lacz / Imagebroker (cra); Jaynes Gallery / DanitaDelimont (clb); Andrew Kandel (cra). 86—87 Alamy Stock Photo: Ronald Wittek / mauritius images GmbH. 87 Dreamstime.com: Natalia Bachkova (cra); Isselee (bl). 88 Alamy Stock Photo: Michelle Himes South (bl/leaf). Dreamstime.com: Natalia Bachkova (bl); Thanakon Niamchaona (cr). 89 Alamy Stock Photo: Sabena Jane Blackbird (cra). Dreamstime.com: Gardendreamer (cla); Elena Shitikova (bl). 90 Alamy Stock Photo: Coyote-Photography.co.uk (bl); Jason Smalley Photography (cr). Dreamstime.com: Gerald Marella (tr). 91 Alamy Stock Photo: fotolincs (cla). Dreamstime.com: Danil Rudenko (cl). Getty Images: Dan Kitwood / Staff (cra). 92 Dreamstime.com: Steve Byland (clb); Mikhail Strogalev (c). 93 Alamy Stock Photo: Jim Laws (cra/Flower). Dreamstime.com: Ghosterz Arts (tl); Mikhail Strogalev (cra); Goldution (tr); Sergey Tolmachyov (br). Getty Images / iStock: E+ / Chushkin (cra/blue butterfly); proxyminder (tr/butterfly). Cover images: Front: Alamy Stock Photo: Design Pics / Radius Images (bc); Dreamstime.com: Charles Brutlag (cra); Melinda Fawver (bl); Mark Hrycil (clb); Isselee (crb); Natalie Schorr (clb/bug); Seth Schubert (tr); Zepherwind (tl); Shutterstock.com: yvontrep (tc). Back: Dreamstime.com: Shhaase (cra); Helen Davies (cb); John Anderson (cb); Rod Hill (cla); Marcelkudla (clb/caterpillar); Paul Reeves (cr); Shutterstock.com: Carl Allen (ca). Spine: 123RF.com: alekss. All other images © Dorling Kindersley